Valerie joon (Dear, soul, life)
enjoy, enjoy, and enjoy, the way you
enjoy life and give joy to your
friends!
    FF   9/6/97

On Entering the Sea

On Entering the Sea

The Erotic and Other Poetry
of Nizar Qabbani

Translated from the Arabic by
Lena Jayyusi and Sharif Elmusa

with

Jack Collom, Diana Der Hovanessian,
John Heath-Stubbs, W.S. Merwin, Christopher
Middleton, Naomi Shihab Nye and Jeremy Reed

Introduction by Salma Khadra Jayyusi

INTERLINK BOOKS
An imprint of Interlink Publishing Group, Inc.
NEW YORK

First published in 1996 by

INTERLINK BOOKS
An imprint of Interlink Publishing Group, Inc.
99 Seventh Avenue • Brooklyn, New York 11215

English translation copyright © Salma Khadra Jayyusi, 1996
Original Arabic copyright © Nizar Qabbani 1980, 1986, 1995

This translation was prepared by PROTA, Project of Translation from
Arabic Literature, founded and directed by Salma Khadra Jayyusi.

Library of Congress Cataloging-in-Publication Data

Qabbānī, Nizār.
    On entering the sea: the erotic and other poetry of Nizar Qabbani /
translated by Lena Jayyusi . . . [et al.].
        p. cm.
    ISBN 1–56656–186–8 — ISBN 1–56656–193–0 (pb)
    1. Qabbānī, Nizār—Translations into English. I. Jayyusi, Lena.
II. Title.
PJ7858.A206 1996
892'.716—dc20   94–47592
                                                             CIP

Printed and bound in the United States of America

10 9 8 7 6 5 4 3 2 1

Contents

i

Poems Translated by Sharif Elmusa and Naomi Shihab Nye

Introduction

Nizar Qabbani: A Lover for All Times

by Salma Khadra Jayyusi

Fifty years on the road of Love
but the road is still unknown
Fifty years, O book of Love,
and still on the first page.[1]

During the twentieth century, Arabic culture has known several writers who made it their mission to transform the world around them. The Arab awakening to modern life at the opening of the century created a new awareness of many possibilities. But, because of the tenacious force of traditions and inherited attitudes, these possibilities remained for too long only partially explored. It took the work of a number of major thinkers and creative writers to throw off some of the psychological shackles and inject new, refreshing ideas and attitudes that set free again the sources of life and vitality in the Arab nation. These resolute pioneers strove to change, often radically, traditional situations, attitudes, concepts, and beliefs prevalent throughout the contemporary culture of the Arab world, the result of several centuries of stagnation and stupor.

Among these rare pioneers is the poet Nizar Qabbani. He comes from a conservative family in Damascus, a city steeped in traditions and established in an urbanity many centuries old, a city that boasts beautiful women, dainty and fragrant as the flowers that hang from its windows or fill its old patios, a city of song, of joyful love of life, of vitality and energy, yet also of entrenched habits and customs, of a well-established way of life, of ancient literary and linguistic traditions.

Some of the pioneering writers made their attack on

the political, social, or religious establishments: Amin al-Raihani (1876–1940) and Gibran Kahlil Gibran (1883–1931) were two of the earliest and noblest. Although the social and political have not escaped his sharp pen, Qabbani's major battle, for which he will be long remembered, has been against the taboos imposed on women and love. The well-aimed attacks of the pioneers aroused consciousness and often restiveness, but it was Qabbani's vociferous and persistent campaign, made mainly through poetry, the medium which has always captured Arab imagination and aroused personal and collective emotions, that has been able to touch the hearts and minds of thousands of women all over the Arab world.

Qabbani was not embracing fashionable causes when he began his concentrated attack on the way women were induced, through a narrow conservative education, to deny their own humanity. He began his campaign long before feminism in the Arab world became a fashionable pursuit. It was through his erotic verse that Qabbani first discovered, for himself and others, the full meaning of freedom, the fact that genuine freedom is not divisible, and cannot be sought except in its totality. Political freedom has been championed by every poet who mattered in the Arab world. In fact, it is virtually impossible for any Arab poet to win esteem among the audience of poetry without first championing the cause of freedom and political liberty. The Arab world is full of poets and other creative writers who are refugees from their own governments because of their audacity in facing up to injustice and repression. This kind of struggle against internal coercion, waged constantly by generation after generation of Arab creative writers, particularly the poets, has long been their privilege and choice, making itself felt before political thinkers begin to wage war through intellectual reasoning and didactic argument. Qabbani's superior achievement, however, is that he not only attacked political coercion, but aimed his well-honed pen at the most sacrosanct taboos in Arab traditional culture: the sexual. He called for the liberation of both body and soul from the repressive injunctions imposed upon them throughout the centuries, awakening women to a new awareness of their bodies and their sexuality, wrenching them away from the taboos of society, and making them aware of its discriminatory treatment of the sexes, of its inherent cruelty. Aroused consciousness is irreversible, except through delusion. Fanatical counterattacks, made in the name of religion, honor, or any of the great absolutes, can warp meaning already gained and re-encode its signals, but they cannot obliterate knowledge already acquired. Something will abide: if not full conviction, at least a question, a lingering doubt. The Qabbani baptism is like a tattoo on the spirit. It cannot be removed.

This is because it addresses the pertinent needs of the body and the heart, engaging the most private, the most pressing, fracturing the built-in taboos, liberating the inner self, forcing hidden passion out of its dark primordial caves, and releasing sexuality and private joy. How can this ever be eradicated from one's inner knowledge? Many women, particularly the younger generations, have treated Qabbani's words as a gospel for feminine liberation. Some have not had the audacity and the vigor of spirit to acknowledge their own autonomy, and have turned Qabbani's songs inward, into their daydreams. But so many more have found their way to a new confidence in their own autonomy and volition, in their inherent right to reject their centuries-old deprivation.

It was the image of the "pure" woman, of whom, to rephrase a famous proverb, it might be said, "no one had ever touched on the cheek with a feather, except her mother," that enraged Qabbani, particularly because it was men who controlled women's destinies and suffocated their humanity. His rebellion was the most vociferous cry against male tyranny. And it brought Arab women face to face with their own predicament. The newly discovered internal authority of the woman, dormant for centuries, was evoked through beautiful words created in a most elaborate Arab poetic idiom—deeply fixed in the memory, and delivered in rhythmic utterance still intoxicating to Arabs everywhere, a medium persuasive in the extreme. Nothing before had been so perfectly able, as this poetry was, to narrate to woman the story of her plight, not film, not fiction, not media: these were either taken as pure figments of the imagination or dubbed as foreign, not worthy of the Arab woman.

The fanatical stress on woman's sexual integrity has a long tradition in Arabic culture. It has made any encroachment on her "purity" a breach not only of her personal honor, but of that of her male relations. In fact, her honor is not simply personal, but part of the family reputation and status; betraying it can trigger immense violence and fierce retribution, because it reflects on the family, or the tribe. Was it the taking of women as hostage in the pre-Islamic raids, tying the dishonor of defeat to the subjugation of the female members of the tribe, that spread its dark cloud over women forever? Nothing wounded the Arab man, always priding himself on his courage, more than the stigma of being unable to defend his women from being taken hostages by the enemy. The pre-Islamic poet, Antara, puts it in telling words:

> In al-Faruq, we safeguarded our women
> warding off the charging horsemen.[2]

Whatever the reason for this extremist concept of "honor," it has become entrenched in the culture. Woman's sexual integrity suffered the strongest taboo, and, with the later influx of non-Arab slave girls through the Islamic conquests, it became more and more severe, as it aimed at strictly separating the "licentious" slave girls from the well-protected "free" Arab women. From that time on, erotic gaiety became the prerogative of slave girls, and would be regarded as profane and demeaning to the "free" Arab woman who now entered the drab and dark ages of her history. Thus, the whole concept of freedom and slavery was inverted, turning the "free" woman into a slave of society's moral distinctions. It was the greatest deception in women's history anywhere. The preservation of the Arab woman's honor became an obsession, involving the imposition of ever harsher measures. It was no longer simply a matter of moral choice, but became the one moral trait that was never left to volition: it was violated only as an act of surrender to instinct, in many instances, where detected, punishable by death. This extreme fanaticism is found in other cultures as well (Kazantzakis' *Zorba, the Greek*, is a good example), but it has been greatest and most protracted in Arabic culture. This colored the whole history of out-of-wedlock relations for Arab women, and was linked with a very deep-rooted fear: the cutting fear of shame and disdain, of losing face and pride, the fear for life, for survival in society. This fear became an instinct in both women and men, and it remained, even up to modern times, an obsessive threat to all women's rapport with love and sexuality. Arabic culture, it must be remembered, is a shame, not a guilt, culture. If guilt can be rationalized away to create excuses for acts of abuse (colonialism and slavery are rationalized as a means of civilizing less cultivated races and peoples), you cannot rationalize shame, particularly the breach of woman's honor. As the Arab proverb has it, "Like a crack in glass, it cannot be mended."

Naturally, the Arab woman continued to inspire men, and there were some periods, as in the golden age of Andalusian poetry (ninth–eleventh century AD), when even women poets would break through the taboos to

ix

announce the merging of virtue with desire. But the majority of women remained the prisoners of their sex, particularly during the four hundred years of the Ottoman period that ended in the Arab world with the end of the First World War.

To remove the shame that hangs on all erotic relations, this was Qabbani's towering achievement.

* * * * * * * * * * * * * *

By far the most popular poet in the Arab world, Qabbani's long tribute to love and feminine beauty is an exceptional feat, unmatched to my knowledge by any other poet in any language. Writing in a verse that is as exhilarating and arduous as it is eloquent and refined, he is one of the great love poets of the world. He certainly is the greatest in Arabic, a language that boasts numerous bards dedicated to the erotic experience. Qabbani is unique as the perennial voice of love and the fervent worshipper of beauty. Erotic involvement for him is a positive pursuit, alive with passion and rapture, full of flair and excitement. His sense of feminine beauty is linked with corporeal desire and evokes in him an insatiability for physical love. He speaks not of parting and unrequited passions but of the harmonious union of man and woman, which alone is the source of life and continuity. This is not in line either with the classical Arab lovers of the Umayyad period (661–750), or with our modern romantics in the twenties and thirties, who concentrated on the pangs of longing and unrequited love, motifs well entrenched in Arabic love poetry (including folk poetry):

> Love, our meeting was strange,
> > and we parted, each a stranger to the other
> I would take refuge in my tears
> > but find only flame instead.[3]

This negative, pining love of earlier poets was alien to Qabbani. Alien to him, too, was the love poetry of the symbolists in the thirties and forties, for whom beauty was a quest for itself; a poetry which, while evoking love, deferred forever the corporeal union, as in Sa'id 'Aql, the greatest of the modern Arab symbolists:

> You're near to me, but are an inviolable temple
> to be touched and visited from afar.

or this:

> Withhold my love, withhold, till that day comes
> when the eye wakes no more, and the playful
> cease to play.

or this:

> Do not approach me, love, but remain
> a lovely idea for my tomorrow.[4]

Qabbani has his roots in the passionate élan of pre-Islamic and Abbasid times, in Andalusian intoxication with the beauty of the beloved. The absence of the erotic in the following by a contemporary woman poet, where the ecstasy seems to arise solely from the sheer beauty of the man addressed and is therefore a purely aesthetic rapture, is foreign to Qabbani's poetry:

> Is it in vain that Shudan passed my way and
> by exquisite beauty lit a beauty within
> that troubles me still?

In this poem, the soul is deeply stirred, yet the sexual desire does not interfere in the reaction caused by the "dazzling" image beheld. No attempt is made to establish contact:

He entered my world, a stranger taking no part
never stealing into my house of memory
winning the honored place among my loves.
Shudan came and went, we never spoke a word!

The meaning of this chance meeting is quite clear to the poet. There can be no erotic consequences: "He'll never kiss those tears I never shed for him." But it is these moments of encounter with beauty, when the aesthetic experience is real and poignant, that nourish the poet's life:

These times give meaning to my life and make me whole
My cup has many cracks, yet the wine always kisses the brim.[5]

Qabbani, on the other hand, is forever the refined predator, endowed with a powerful instinct constantly driving him toward woman. He, too, is a great lover of beauty and his eye pries for beauty with great exigency. The search for a companion to his body and soul has been the most ardent pursuit throughout his life, but a pursuit bridled by an exacting covenant: that his heart should be engaged only when his eye is entranced. It is then that the aesthetic merges with the erotic to the point of perfection, and it is then that the song of celebration begins, enchanting, ennobling, stirring desire, and awakening the dreams of the heart. And it continues, rhythmic and colorful, exploring all the treasures of the beloved, groping to reach her most profound essence where the sources of her passions lie. The echoes of these songs, brimming with primordial joy, tear through the layers of old beliefs and taboos, renaming things, giving new definitions to corporeal desire:

Disrobe, my love,
Since it has been such
a long time since the time

of miracles. Disrobe.
And let miracles begin.
I am speechless before you.
Your body speaks all languages.

The stifled life of the Arab woman did not strike
Qabbani as evil in the early days of his career. Like many
other members of his urban culture, endowed with
comeliness and fine taste and fortunate enough to enjoy
some leisure, he was the perfect Don Juan on the lookout
for beautiful women. He was even somewhat traditional
at times, an Arab man affirming his own potency and
machismo. When I wrote about his poetry in 1957, I said
that he loved beauty and women, but was never captured
by love. He replied, in a private letter that I still have,
confirming this. But he has come a long way since, fully
experiencing the joy of great love, and suffering
profoundly at its sudden cruel interruption, when his
wife, a lovely woman of great serenity and poise, died
violently in the rubble of a terrorist attack in Beirut.
However, the forces of life were stronger than death,
and after an initial period of grief, his heart was in
remission again, and erotic excitement reasserted itself in
verses of shimmering beauty:

My first mistake
(and not my last)
was to live
in the state of wonder
ready to be amazed
by the simple span
of night and day,
and ready for every woman
I loved to break me
into a thousand pieces. . . .

His writings on love explore all aspects of the love

experience in an amazing multiplicity of forms. Read in its entirety, his poetry becomes a prayer in homage to love. Although the physical is never forgotten, there is an abundant emotional *élan* that cannot help but awaken the senses to spiritual fulfillment. It is as if when painting the body, he also paints the spirit, and, through erotic communion, the road from the body to the spirit is traversed. Yet, despite his involvement with physical love, he treats all his subjects with enough artistic flair to remove any hint of the pornographic. Even his treatment of a lesbian relationship, which is not generally accepted openly as a legitimate erotic activity, paints a truly artistic picture of the two female lovers involved in the love act.[6] Moreover, his poetry expresses no hedonism, for he elevates where he loves, and, being an act of positive involvement, it also does not reflect any dolorism. When he is wounded, he does not react plaintively, but responds with anger and protest, as when his wife was killed. It can be argued that genuine sorrow is a legitimate reaction to loss in love: those with a profound insight into the universal human condition know that it harbors the possibility of loss even at the most triumphant moments of love and union. However, Qabbani's poetry could not have been the true antidote to the grief and despair of our romantic poets just before him had his nature been different. Thus, it remained the answer to a deep need in the age to shake off any lingering dolorism and bring life, joy, rubustness, and courage to the love relation.

Qabbani's fifty-year experiment is the proof of love's capacity to assert itself even in an age of chaos and tragedy, to assume its potential joy even in the face of all the catastrophes that have afflicted the contemporary Arab world. He started his poetic career in the forties, at a time when there was still much hope of the possibility of resurgence and the capacity of the Arab nation to assert its freedom and to prevail. However, Qabbani soon

became more and more involved in both the social and
the political situation, and recognized the predicament of
Arab life for what it was: the result of external
aggression, local tyrannies, and, above all, political
naiveté. It was mainly through his involvement with
woman that he discovered, at the outset of the fifties,
how very oppressed and suppressed she was, and how
tyrannical the injunctions against her life were; by the end
of the sixties, he had assumed his strong role as her
prime defender.

It was also at the end of the sixties that his political
involvement assumed its fullest form. Of the three
large volumes comprising his poetic oeuvre, one is
completely dedicated to his political poetry. After the
Arab defeat in the June War of 1967, he became one of
the most eloquent political poets in the Arab world. It is
a painful testimony to the many upheavals the Arab
world has experienced in the last fifty years that the poet
of ecstasy and celebration, of joy and bliss, was forced
out of the bower of love into the open arena of Arab
politics, and, immediately after the June War, he said as
much:

> Ah my country! You have transformed me
> from a poet of love and yearning
> to a poet writing with a knife.

And just as he celebrated love, he condemned with equal
passion the tragic flaws in contemporary Arab culture
that he felt made defeat possible. He wrote the angriest
poem in contemporary Arabic, "Notes on the Book of the
Defeat," in the aftermath of the June War. After that,
poems of biting satire, of bitter social and political
invective followed, one after the other, all written in a
language accessible to all and memorized by millions.[7] A
daring invective, a deep anger, and sharp critical insight
characterize his political work.

xv

His Andalusian poems, written when he was a diplomat in Spain, reflect his absolute reverence for beauty and his celebration of his own culture and the memory of its great civilization in medieval times, when the Arabs ruled in Andalusia for eight centuries. He saw in Spain, in the dark eyes of Andalusian beauties, in the locks of their hair, in the patios of houses and their inner fountains flowing with water, in the heart-rending tunes of the flamenco echoing the folk songs of the Arab countryside, in the grace and hospitality and generous merriment of the Andalusians, living reminders of his Arab ancestors who stayed there for eight hundred years.

> At noon the streets of Granada
> are fields of black pearls
> From where I sit
>
> I see my country with wide eyes—
> the minarets of Damascus
> depicted on every braid of hair.
> ("Spanish Leaves")

And it is touching to see that, aside from his elegy on his son, a promising young man whose death was devastating to the poet, the only time his poetry betrays profound sorrow, unmitigated by protest or political rage, is in his Andalusian poems. It is on these occasions, one feels, that the poet of eternal hope is faced with the despair of a final loss.

But despite this patriotic involvement, well revealed in his Andalusian poems, which carried a fervor deeply moving to the Arab spirit everywhere, and despite the effectiveness and timeliness of his political poems, he remains, first and foremost, the poet of love and beauty. His love poetry transcends the realm of the personal to describe the perennial, never-dying spring of human love, to join the individual to the universal and the particular

xvi

to the absolute. However, although he is a lover for all times, he is also a lover for the present time. He has set the timeless love experience within the possibilities and needs of the epoch, strongly rejecting contemporary chaos and all forms of present-day tyranny, but, at the same time, strongly rejecting despair and death and imparting a message of life and hope in asserting love's capacity to prevail.

Notes

1. This is an overture to Qabbani's collection *Painting With Words* (1966). I have changed the original "twenty" to "fifty."
2. "Al-Faruq" is a place name.
3. Ibrahim Naji, 1898–1953 (Egypt), from his poem, "The End of All Nights," *Diwan Naji* (Cairo, 1961), p. 147.
4. All three example are from his collection *Rindala* (Beirut, 1950), the first from his poem, "I Love You," p. 25; the second from "Do Not Confess"; and the third from "Brunette," p. 120.
5. From a poem by Salma K. Jayyusi entitled "Shudan," published in *Women of the Fertile Crescent*, ed. Kamal Boullata (Washington DC, 1978). "Shudan" is an Indian name.
6. "Evil Poem," in his collection *Poems* (1956).
7. This critical political stance has intensified with the years, and Qabbani has come to react with increasing dismay to what he sees as the continuous national disintegration and the disunity of purpose that characterize the Arab world today. He also expresses great abhorrence for the greed and the materialism that have demeaned human relations, as well as for the mounting fundamentalism and the narrowing outlook that threaten to wipe away the modernist achievements gained by the Arabs throughout the twentieth century. In a recent poem, "When Will They Announce the Death of the Arabs" (published in *Al-Hayat* periodical, No. 11576, October 28, 1994) he expressed, in fiery words, his rage and despair at contemporary Arab life. This brought about many counterattacks by conservatives in the Arab world, to which the poet responded, with his usual verve and eloquence. It testifies to the general malaise afflicting the contemporary Arab world that this most generous and patriotic of poets, with almost thirty books of poetry to his name, who has only ever wished for progress and freedom for his people, should be made the butt of fanatical rage at this phase of his life.

Poems Translated by
Lena Jayyusi and Jack Collom

The Book of Love

Your love, eyes of a doe,
Is the extreme, the mystical;
It is worship itself.
Your love, like birth and death,
Is difficult to repeat.

*

All that they say about me is true;
All they say about my reputation
In love, with women ... is true,
But they did not learn
That I bleed in your love
Like Christ.

*

Don't worry, most beautiful,
You're always in my words and in my verses.
You may grow older, as you go,
But never on my pages.

*

It is not enough that you were born beautiful.
You had to pass through my arms one day
To be more than beautiful.

*

When I travel within your eyes, my darling,
I feel I am riding a magic carpet.
A rose-colored cloud lifts me up,
Then a violet one.
I spin in your eyes, my love;

3

I spin ... like the earth.

*

How you resemble a little fish,
Timid in love ... like a fish.
But you killed a thousand women inside me
And became Queen.

*

Undress ... for a very long time
No miracles have fallen on this earth.
Strip naked ... disrobe.
I am mute—
Your body knows all languages.

*

When I love
I become time
Out of time.

*

I wrote on the wind
The name of my love.
I wrote it on the water.
I did not know
That the wind rushes by without listening,
That names dissolve in the water.

*

You still ask me the date of my birth.
Write this down,
And now you know: my birthday

4

Occurred when you began to love me.

*

Should the djinn come out
Of his bottle and say,
"At your service, Sir!
You have one minute to choose
Priceless emeralds from all the world,"
I would choose only your eyes.

*

I melted in my love all the pens—
The blue ... the red ... the green ...
Until the words were formed.
I hung my love on the bracelets of doves
And did not know
That they both fly away.

Testimony of Guarantee

You want a testimony of love from me
Signed in big letters?
I declare that you are
The last among women.
But why the testimony? Tell me,
Can the sea guarantee forever
The boundaries of an island?

On Entering the Sea

Love happened at last,
And we entered God's paradise,
Sliding
Under the skin of the water
Like fish.
We saw the precious pearls of the sea
And were amazed.
Love happened at last
Without intimidation ... with symmetry of wish.
So I gave ... and you gave
And we were fair.
It happened with marvelous ease
Like writing with jasmine water,
Like a spring flowing from the ground.

Maritime Poem

In the blue harbor of your eyes
Blow rains of melodious lights,
Dizzy suns and sails
Painting their voyage to endlessness.

In the blue harbor of your eyes
Is an open sea window,
And birds appear in the distance
Searching for islands still unborn.

In the blue harbor of your eyes
Snow falls in July.
Ships laden with turquoise
Spill over the sea and are not drowned.

In the blue harbor of your eyes
I run on the scattered rocks like a child
Breathing the fragrance of the sea
And return an exhausted bird.

In the blue harbor of your eyes
Stones sing in the night.
Who has hidden a thousand poems
In the closed book of your eyes?

If only, if only I were a sailor,
If only somebody'd give me a boat,
I would furl my sails each evening
In the blue harbor of your eyes.

When I Love You

When I love you
A new language springs up,
New cities, new countries discovered.
The hours breathe like puppies,
Wheat grows between the pages of books,
Birds fly from your eyes with tidings of honey,
Caravans ride from your breasts carrying Indian herbs,
The mangoes fall all around, the forests catch fire
And Nubian drums beat.

When I love you your breasts shake off their shame,
Turn into lightning and thunder, a sword, a sandy storm.
When I love you the Arab cities leap up and demonstrate
Against the ages of repression
And the ages
Of revenge against the laws of the tribe.
And I, when I love you,
March against ugliness,
Against the kings of salt,
Against the institutionalization of the desert.
And I shall continue to love you until the world flood
   arrives;
I shall continue to love you until the world flood arrives.

I am afraid

I am afraid to tell my beloved
That I love her;
Jugged wine
Loses something when it's poured out.

*Poems Translated by
Lena Jayyusi and Diana Der
Hovanessian*

Two African Breasts

Let me find time
to welcome in this love
that comes unbid.
Let me find time
to memorize
this face that rises
out of the trees
of forgetfulness.
Give me the time
to escape this love
that stops my blood.
Let me find time
to recognize your name,
my name,
and the place
where I was born.
Let me find time
to know where I shall die
and how I will revive, as
a bird inside your eyes.
Let me find time
to study the state of winds
and waves, to learn the maps
of bays . . .

Woman, who lodges
inside the future
pepper and pomegranate seeds,
give me a country
to make me forget all countries,
and give me time
to avoid this Andalusian face,
this Andalusian voice,
this Andalusian death
coming from all directions.

Let me find time to prophesy
the coming of the flood.

Woman, who was inscribed
in books of magic,
before you came
the world was prose.
Now poetry is born.
Give me the time to catch
the colt that runs toward me,
your breast.
The dot over a line.
A bedouin breast, sweet
as cardamom seeds
as coffee brewing over embers,
its form ancient as Damascene brass
as Egyptian temples.

Let me find luck
to pick the fish that swim
under the waters.

Your feet on the carpet
are the shape and stance
of poetry.

Let me find the luck
to know the dividing line
between the certainty
of love and heresy.
Give me the opportunity
to be convinced I have seen
the star, and have been spoken to
by saints.

Woman, whose thighs are like
the desert palm that golden

dates fall from,
your breasts speak seven tongues
and I was made to listen
to them all.
Give me the chance
to avoid this storm,
this sweeping love,
this wintry air, and to be convinced,
to blaspheme, and to enter
the flesh of things.
Give me the chance
to be the one
to walk on water

Painting With Words

Twenty years on the road of love
but the road is still unmapped.
Sometimes I was the victor.
More often the vanquished.
Twenty years, O book of love
and still on the first page.

The Child Scribbles

My fault, my greatest fault,
O sea-eyed princess,
was to love you
as a child loves.
(The greatest lovers,
after all, are children.)

My first mistake
(and not my last)
was to live
in the taste of wonder
ready to be amazed
by the simple span
of night and day,

and ready for every woman
I loved to break me
into a thousand pieces to make
me an open city,
and to leave me behind her
as dust.

My weakness was to see
the world with the logic of a child.
And my mistake was dragging
love out of its cave into the open air,
making my breast
an open church for all lovers.

Notes on the Book of Defeat

If an audience could be arranged
and also my safe return
this is what I'd tell the Sultan.
This is what he'd learn:
O Sultan, my master, if my clothes
are ripped and torn
it is because your dogs with claws
are allowed to tear me.
And your informers every day are those
who dog my heels, each step
unavoidable as fate.
They interrogate my wife, at length,
and list each friend's name.
Your soldiers kick and beat me,
force me to eat from my shoes,
because I dare approach these walls
for an audience with you.
You have lost two wars
and no one tells you why.
Half your people have no tongues.
What good their unheard sigh?
The other half, within these walls,
run like rabbits and ants,
silently inside.
If I were given safety
from the Sultan's armed guards
I would say, O Sultan,
the reason you've lost wars twice
was because you've been walled in from
mankind's cause and voice.

I Conquer the World with Words

I conquer the world with words,
conquer the mother tongue,
verbs, nouns, syntax.
I sweep away the beginning of things
and with a new language
that has the music of water the message of fire
I light the coming age
and stop time in your eyes
and wipe away the line
that separates
time from this single moment.

Foolishness

When I wiped you from
the book of memory
I did not know I was striking
out half my life.

Language

When a man is in love
how can he use old words?
Should a woman
desiring her lover
lie down with
grammarians and linguists?

I said nothing
to the woman I loved
but gathered
love's adjectives into a suitcase
and fled from all languages.

Cup and Rose

I went to the coffeehouse
intending to forget
our love and bury
my sorrows, but
you emerged
from the bottom of my
coffee cup,
a white rose.

Equation

I love you
therefore I am
in the present.
I write, beloved,
and retrieve the past.

The Actors

When ideas, when thought itself,
flattens out, in a city,
and curves like a horseshoe,
when any rifle picked up by
a coward can crush a man,
when an entire city becomes
a trap, and its people turn
into mice,
when the newspapers become mere
funeral notices,
everything dies
everything is without life —
the water, the plants,
voices and colors.
Trees migrate, leaving their roots.
Geography is wrested
from its place; place escapes
and we see the end of man.

*

When a helmet becomes God in heaven
and can do what it wishes
with a citizen — crush, mash
kill and resurrect
whatever it wills,
then the state is a whorehouse,
history is a rag,
and thought is lower than boots.

When a breath of air
comes by decree
of the sultan,
when every grain of wheat we eat,
every drop of water we drink

24

comes only by decree
of the sultan,
when an entire nation turns into
a herd of cattle fed in the sultan's
shed, embryos will suffocate
in the womb, women will miscarry
and the sun will drop
a black noose over our square.

*

The June war is over.
It is as if nothing happened.
Faces, eyes are no different.
The courts of Inquisition reopened
and the inspectors, the Don Quixotes,
are back with their malignant conclusions.
People laugh
because it is past crying
They laugh because
it is beyond tears.
And we are content,
content with war, with peace,
with heat, with cold,
content with sterility, with
fertility, and with everything
in the Book of Fate
in the Heavens. And all we can say is
"Unto God we shall return."

*

The stage is burned
down to the pit
but the actors have not died yet.

25

*Poems Translated by
Lena Jayyusi and John
Heath-Stubbs*

Opening Poem

In the beginning there were poems. And I suppose
that the exception then was flat bald prose
First of all there was the deep wide sea
dry land exception then appeared to be
First the breast's abundant curve and all
the plainer contours were exceptional
And first of all was you and only you
then afterwards were other women too.

Diary of an Indifferent Woman

I am a woman
I am a woman
The day I came into this world
I found my extermination was decreed
But I never saw the doors of law courts
nor the faces of my judges.

*

The hands of the clock
are like the jaws of a whale, ready to swallow me
—hands like two snakes on the wall
like a guillotine, like a noose
like a knife that rips me apart
like a thief with quick footsteps
following me, following me
Why shouldn't I smash it?
when every one of its minutes smashes me?
I am a woman in whose heart
the pulse of time has stopped
I do not know spring flowers
nor does April know me.

*

Why does my father play the tyrant with me
and wear me down with his authority?
Why does he look upon me as an object,
as a line of print in his newspaper?
Why is he so anxious that I should remain his only
as if I were just part of his property,
something ALWAYS THERE
LIKE A CHAIR IN HIS ROOM?
Is it just good enough to be his daughter?
I reject my father's wealth

30

his pearls and silver
My father never once noticed
my body and its rebellion
Selfish
sick in his love,
sick in his fanaticism
sick in his domineering
He is enraged if he sees my breasts
have become fuller and more rounded;
he is enraged if he sees a man
approach that garden
But my father can never prevent the apples
completing their circle
A thousand birds will come
and rob his orchard.

*

I love the birds of October
they travel wherever they wish
carrying in their suitcases
what is left of the almonds and figs
to get lost like the October birds
Sweet it is to get lost so.

Every now and then
I would wish to seek a homeland
a new homeland . . . not inhabited
and for a God who does not keep on pursuing me
and a land that will not become my enemy
I want to escape from my own skin
from my own voice, from my own language
and stray like the fragrance of gardens
I want to flee from my own shadow
and from all addresses
I want to run away from the East of superstition
    and snakes

31

of caliphs and princes
and of all sultans
I want to love like the October birds
O Eastern lands of halter and knives.

*

I ask myself continually
why should love in this world not be for all,
like the light of the dawn
Why should not love be like bread and wine
and like the water of the river
and like the clouds and the rains
the grasses and the flowers?
Is not love for humanity
a life within a life?
Why can't love in this country of mine be spontaneous,
just like a white flower
blooming from the rock
spontaneous as the encounter of lips with lips
flowing free like the hair on my back
why can't people love easily and naturally?
like fish swimming in the sea,
like the stars moving in their spheres
Why can't love in this country of mine be as essential
as a book of poems?

*

Why is love in our city
contraband and counterfeit?
We snatch at promises through chinks in the door
and have to beg for letters
or for little scrolls
Why in our city
do they shoot down feelings as they shoot down birds?
Why are we like base metal?

32

What is left of man if he is base metal?
Why are we two-faced about our thoughts and feelings?
mundane, underhanded, afraid of the light and the sun?
Why are the people of our city
torn apart by contradictions?
For in their waking hours
they curse braided hair and they curse skirts
and when night enfolds them
they embrace nude pictures.

My brother comes back from the whorehouse
at dawn, drunk as a lord
but he remains, in the eyes of the family,
the apple of their eyes
and—even in his lust and bawdry—
they see him as the purest of the pure
My brother returns from the whorehouse
proud and strutting like a cock
Praise be to God who created him out of light
and us out of vile cinders
and blessed be He who wipes away his sins
and does not wipe out ours.

*

I'll speak of my girl companions
I see my own story
in that of each of them
and the same tragedy
I'll write about my girl companions
about the prison that saps their lives
about the time wasted in reading women's magazines
about the never-opened doors
about desires nipped in the bud
about the nipples screaming out beneath the silk
about the great prison cell
and its black walls

33

about the thousands and thousands of martyred girls
buried in nameless graves in the cemetery of tradition
These friends of mine are like dolls swathed in cotton
inside a locked museum
like coins, minted by history, that can neither be spent
nor given away
shoals of fish suffocated in their ponds
crystal bottles with dead butterflies in them
I shall write about my friends fearlessly
about the blood-stained fetters on the feet of beautiful
    girls
about their hallucinations, their nausea and about nights
    of entreaty to God
about desires stifled in the pillows
about going round and round in the void
about the death of fleeting moments
My friends are slaves bought and sold in superstition's
    market
captives in an Eastern harem, dead without being dead
they live and die like mushrooms under glass
My friends
birds who perish in caves without a single sound.

Cashmere Down

This is no season now for thought
  I am not made of wood, alas,
Nor are those soft lips of yours
  of hard and polished brass

Your little hand in mine is like
  a delicate silken handkerchief
Your body's charms are countless and
  this life of ours is brief.

This is no time for thinking, dear,
  the only skill that I call mine—
It is the writing of my poems
  Thinking is not my line.

Peace upon you, blossoming lilies
  falling from heaven in a shower
Soft as down or cashmere silk
  Blessings be your dower.

Your body's naked as a sword blade
  and your breasts set me afire
so that I fly to marvelous heights
  of fancy and desire.

Peace upon you, isles of crystal
  sweet to die upon your breast
since explanations murder love
  not to ask is best.

I love you and my memory's numb
  What I am I do not know
what I was and what shall be
  and whither I should go.

I love you though that love should lead
    to the destruction of my soul
Walking as does a Buddhist monk
    who treads on red hot coal.

This is the age of change and wonder
    Let us flee then, you and I
The headman's sword and old wives tales
    from both of them we'll fly.

Draw near, draw near, and let us go
    shattering all a thousand fold
for there's no building things anew
    till we've destroyed the old.

From your body then shall come
    every foray of the free
Let your body be the source
    of all our liberty

You Cannot Be Accounted Fair

You cannot be accounted fair, not by
the canons whereby men would measure beauty
You can't be deemed intriguing in the way
men speak of charm and of seductiveness
Not dangerous indeed if that implies
that it is woman seals the fate of men
But there's a thing about you, mystical
strange and poetic, full of sexual power
urging me onwards still so that I frame
thousands of wild and giddy suppositions
Lovely I will not call you, but there's something
pierces my very manhood to the core
like the bouquet of wine or orange blossom
something surprising me, burning and drowning
until it seems that I am wholly lost
between reality and the realm of fancy.
Fair I'll not deem you, yet you have an air
that's watery, childlike, something of the city
something of Iraq or of Damascus
that speaks to me, and yet withholds all answers.

Dialogue

They ask me whom I love, I answer
I have not seen her face. Although
for twice ten centuries I've loved her,
her name I do not know.

The Trial

The East receives my songs, some praise, some curse
To each of them my gratitude I bear
For I've avenged the blood of each slain woman
and haven offered her who is in fear.

Woman's rebellious heart I have supported
ready to pay the prize—content to die
if love should slay me, for I am love's champion
and if I ceased, then I would not be I.

Difficulty

Often have I admired a woman's beauty
and yet my heart was not engaged, for here
upon this earth are many lovely women
and yet to love is difficult, I fear.

What Has God to Lose?

What then has God to lose, He who has formed
like a bright apple in the heavens the sun
He who made waters flow, and mountains fixed
What has He got to lose, if just for fun
He changed our natures making me less ardent
and you less beautiful to look upon.

In Memory of Taha Husain

Light of your eyes I view, two stars may be:
Among us all it's you alone can see.

Eons of years endured the words I bear
But through the smoke clouds can you see them there?

Would we might sit together in some nook
and there the storehouse of our grief unlock

All ages shall be present then and known
for to the writer each age is his own

Sir, you have made day out of night and all
the whole wide world a joyous festival

You've seized the sun and on it you have thrown
the richly crimson garment that's your own

A river you, who gave us water sweet
and clothed us with the rose and marguerite

Like honey on my tongue the words you write
making the whole world drunken with delight

It's you unveiled the soul, to penetrate
our moral darkness and our bankrupt state

The one who snatched the fire from heaven was you
and all time's frontiers you have broken through

Now thought is changed to spurious politics
the man of letters plays a jester's tricks

Who knows what's now become of poetry
It's part delusion, part insanity.

Return to us once more, for you can save
from the fierce flood and overwhelming wave

You taught us to defy, to break the bars
and grind down to the dust the shining stars

We sloughed our skin, with our own hands tore down
the cosmos and its ramparts of hard stone.

We spurned earth's tyrants nor would bend the knee
to idols and their false divinity

The soul is most oppressed and burdened when
it is the hands of cowards wield the pen.

43

Poems Translated by
Lena Jayyusi and W.S. Merwin

Love under House Arrest

I ask your leave to go
for the blood I used to think would never turn to water
has turned to water
and the sky whose blue crystal I used to think
could not break . . . has broken
and the sun
which I used to hang in your ear
like a Spanish earring
has fallen from me to the ground . . . and smashed
and the words
I used to cover you with when you slept
have fled like frightened birds
and left you naked.

A Thousand Moons

You are no ordinary woman
You are astonishment itself . . . the guessing
at what is to come unexpectedly
How is it that in a moment
    of discovery and inspiration
you extract water from the heart of a stone?
How is it that with the touch of an eyelash
you turn the solitary moon
    into a thousand crescents?

Stage Act

Before others I say that you are not my beloved
and deep inside I know what a liar I am
I claim that there is nothing between us
just to keep trouble from us
And sweet as they are, I deny the rumors of love
and make ruins out of my beautiful history.
Stupidly, I declare my innocence
slay my desires, become a monk
kill my fragrance, deliberately
run away from the paradise of your eyes
play the clown, my love
I fail in that role and come back
For the night, even if it wanted to, cannot hide its stars,
nor can the sea, even if it wanted to,
   hide its ships.

Questions to God

My God!
What overcomes us when we love?
What happens deep inside us?
What gets broken within us?
How is it that we revert to childhood when we love?
how is it that a drop of water becomes an ocean
the palm-trees become taller
the water of the sea sweeter
How does the sun become a precious diamond bracelet
when we love?

My God:
When love strikes us unexpectedly
what is it that we let go from us?
What is it that is born in us?
Why do we become like young pupils
naive and innocent?
And why is it that when our beloved laughs
the world rains jasmines on us
why is it that when she weeps upon our knees
the world becomes a doleful bird?

My God:
What is it called, that love which century after century
has slain men, conquered fortresses
humbled the mighty
and melted the meek and simple?
How is it that the hair of our beloved becomes
  a bed of gold
and her lips wine and grape?
How is it that we walk through fire
and enjoy the flame?
How do we become captives when we love
after having been victorious kings?

What do we call that love which enters us like a knife?
Is it a headache?
Is it madness?
How is it that in the space of one second
the world becomes
a green oasis ... a tender corner
when we love?

My God:
What happens to our reason?
What happens to us?
How does the moment of longing turn into years
and illusion become certainty in love?
How do the weeks of the year become disjointed?
How is it that love abolishes all seasons?
So summer comes in winter
and roses bloom in the orchards of the sky
when we love?

My God:
How do we surrender to love, give it the keys to our
    sanctuary
carry candles to it, the fragrance of saffron
How is it that we fall at its feet, asking forgiveness
how is it that we seek to enter its domain, surrendering
to all that it does to us
all that it does.

My God:
If you are a true God
then let us forever remain
    lovers.

Insane Poems

Homeland Within a Coat

When it rains in Beirut, I need some tenderness
Enter into my rain-soaked coat
enter into the woolen sweater, into my skin, my voice
grant me a homeland within the gray fur coat
eat, like a mare, from the grass of my breast.

Our Story

Should I leave you? When our story
is sweeter than April's return
more beautiful than a gardenia
in the darkness of Spanish hair.

The Eternal Wanderer

What? Does the distance weary you?
Nothing in your eyes wearies me
I long to be lost,
terrible is the road that does not leave me lost.

Woman with No Address

You will search everywhere for her,
You will ask the waves of the sea about her, the
    turquoise of
the shore,
You will roam sea after sea
Your tears will overflow into rivers
and your sorrow will grow to become trees
and at the end of life
you will know that you have been chasing
a thread of smoke
for your heart's love has no land, no homeland, no
    address.

The Bather

I never told them of you ... but
in my eyes, they caught sight of you bathing.

Unexpected Fishes

I have not loved you till now, but
the inevitable hour of love will come
and the sea will throw fishes you never expected
across your breasts.

Butterfly

In green pencil I drew a line around your waist
so it won't ever think to become a butterfly
and fly off ...

Enough

Your presence is enough for place to cease to be
Your coming is enough for Time never to come.

All of You

Love me, do not
fear the water on your feet
You shall never receive the baptism
of womanhood
as long as your body and your hair
remain outside the water ...

Love

When I fell in love
the Lord's kingdom changed
It changed
The night began to sleep in my coat
and the sun began to rise from the west.

Bracelets

All the bracelets in the world do not fit your hands
except the bracelets of my love.

Without Words

Because the words in the dictionary are dead
I discovered a way
of loving you
                without words.

Orange

Love peels me like an orange
opens my breast at night and leaves:
wine and corn and oil lanterns.
Yet I never remember that I was slain
never remember that I bled
never remember what I saw.

Siesta

Your words are a Persian carpet
Your eyes two Damascene sparrows
    that fly between wall and wall
my heart, like the dove, travels across the waters
    of your hands
and takes a siesta
    beneath the shade of the wall.

Contrary Love

I tried to persuade your hair not to grow
too long over your shoulders
not to be a wall of sadness,
over my life
But your hair disappointed all wishes
and remained long

54

And I advised your body not to rouse the
    mirror's fantasy
but your body disobeyed all counsel
and remained beautiful
And I tried to persuade your love
that a year's vacation
by the sea, or a mountain top
    would benefit us both
but your love flung the suitcases down on the sidewalk
and told me it would not go.

More Beautiful

And woman too is beautiful
and more beautiful still
is the imprint of her feet
across our papers.

With Childhood

I shall not be with your tonight
I shall not be in any place
I have bought ships with violet sails
and trains that stop only at the station
    of your eyes
paper planes that fly by the power of love alone
I have brought paper and crayons
and decided to stay up all night
    with my Childhood.

Vine-Grove

Every man that will kiss you after me
will discover on your lips
a small vine-grove
which I planted.

Embryo

I want to keep you within my body
a child whose birth is impossible
a secret dagger-thrust
which nobody can feel except me.

Winter

I remember your love in winter
and I pray to the rains
   to fall in some other country
to the snow to fall
   over other cities
and to God to abolish the winter from His calendar
I do not know how I will face
the winter after you.

Searching for You

Love is my pursuit
You are my pursuit
Love roams over my skin
you roam over my skin
and I
carry the rain-washed streets and sidewalks
on my back ... and search for you.

Passion

Between your breasts lie villages in ashes
thousands and thousands of mines
the wrecks of drowned ships
the shields of slain men
of whom no word came back
All who passed between your breasts disappeared
and those who remained till morning
   committed suicide

Walking on Water

The most beautiful thing about our love
is that it has no mind or reason
The most beautiful thing about our love
is that it walks on water
    and does not drown.

Geometry

You have no real time outside the boundaries
    of my passion
I am your time
You have no clear dimensions
outside the compass of my arms
I am all your dimensions
your corners . . . your circles
your slopes
and your straight lines.

She Alone

All the women I have known
loved me when they were sober
My mother alone
loved me when she was drunk.

Writing History

Read me . . . so that you may always be proud
Read me . . . each time you search the desert for a drop
    of water
Read me . . . each time they shut the gates of hope in the
    face of lovers
do not write of the sorrows of a single woman
but of the history of all women.

Love Letters

1.

Between us
twenty years of age
between your lips and my lips
when they meet and stay
the years collapse
the glass of a whole life shatters.

2.

The day I met you I tore up
all my maps
all my prophecies
like an Arab stallion I smelled the rain
of you
before it wet me
heard the pulse of your voice
before you spoke
undid your hair with my hands
before you had braided it.

3.

There is nothing I can do
nothing you can do
what can the wound do
with the knife on the way to it?

4.

Your eyes are like a night of rain
in which ships are sinking
and all I wrote is forgotten
In mirrors there is no memory.

5.

God how is it that we surrender
to love giving it the keys to our city

carrying candles to it and incense
falling down at its feet asking
to be forgiven
Why do we look for it and endure
all that it does to us
all that it does to us?

6.

Woman in whose voice
silver and wine mingle
in the rains
From the mirrors of your knees
the day begins its journey
life puts out to sea.

7.

I knew when I said
I love you
that I was inventing a new alphabet
for a city where no one could read
that I was saying my poems
in an empty theater
and pouring my wine
for those who could not
taste it.

8.

When God gave you to me
I felt that He had loaded
everything my way
and unsaid all His sacred books.

9.

Who are you, woman?
You who enter like a dagger into my history
you, gentle-hearted as the eyes of a rabbit
soft as the down of a plum,

you, pure as jasmine necklaces
innocent as children's tunics
savage as words
Get out of the pages of my notebook
get out of the sheets of my bed
get out of the coffee cups
of the spoons of sugar
get out of the buttons of my shirt
and the threads of my handkerchief
get out of my toothbrush
the lather on my face
get out of all my little things
so that I can work. . . .

10.

Your love flung me into the land of wonder
assaulted me
    like the fragrance of a woman
    entering an elevator
surprised me
as I sat with a poem in a coffee-bar
I forgot the poem
surprised me
    reading the lines on my palm
I forgot my palm
accosted me like a wild rooster
that does not see . . . and does not hear,
its feathers mingled with my feathers
its cries mingled with my cries,
surprised me
sitting on my suitcases
waiting for the train of my days
I forgot the train,
forgot the days
and traveled with you
to the Land of Wonder.

11.

Your countenance is engraved on the face of my watch
engraved on the minute hand
engraved on the weeks . . .
the months . . . the years
I no longer have a time of my own
for you have become all of Time.

12.

When you put your head on my shoulder
as I drive my car
the stars leave their orbit
and descend in thousands
to slide over the glass windows . . .
and the moon comes down
to settle on my shoulder.
Then
    smoking with you becomes a pleasure
    conversation a pleasure
    and silence a pleasure.
And losing our way on the wintry roads
    that have no name
    becomes a pleasure.
And I wish . . . that we could stay like that forever
the rain singing
the windshield wipers singing
and your little head
clutching onto the grass of my breast
like a tropical colored butterfly
that refuses to fly off.

13.

I am not a teacher
to teach you how to love
Fish need no teacher
to learn how to swim
and birds need no teacher

to learn how to fly
swim by yourself
fly by yourself
love has no notebooks
and the greatest lovers in history
never knew how to read.

14.
I hum your little bright-colored memories
the way a bird sings
the way the fountain of an Andalusian house
sings
its blue water.

15.
My letters to you
transcend me . . . and transcend you
because the light is
    more important than the lamp,
the poem more important than the notebook,
the kiss more important than the lips.
My letters to you
are more important than you
    more important than me
they are the only documents
in which others shall discover your beauty
and my madness.

16.
Between us
there are twenty-two years of living
Between your lips and mine
when they cling together
the years are crushed
and the glass of a lifetime is shattered.

17.

When I hear men
    talk eagerly of you
and hear women
    talk irritably of you
I know
how beautiful you are.

Twelve Roses in Balqis's Hair

1.

I knew that she would be killed
and she knew that I would be killed
both prophecies came true
she fell, like a butterfly, beneath the rubble of
  (the Age of Ignorance)
and I fell . . . between the fangs of an age
that devoured poems
the eyes of women
and the rose of freedom

2.

I knew that she would be killed
she was beautiful in an age that was ugly
pure in an age that was contaminated
noble in the age of hoodlums
She was a rare pearl
amidst the piles of artificial pearls
a unique woman
amidst the stacks of artificial women

3.

I knew that she would be killed
because her eyes were clear as two emerald rivers
and her hair was long as a *mawwal* of Baghdad
the nerves of this homeland
cannot bear the density of green
cannot bear the sight of a million palm trees
gathering in Balqis's eyes

4.

I knew that she would be killed
for the compass of her pride
was greater than the compass of the Peninsula
Her heritage did not permit her

to live in the age of decadence
her luminary nature
did not permit her to live in the dark

5.

In the intensity of her pride
she believed that the earth was too small for her
so she packed her suitcases
and withdrew on tiptoes
without telling a soul . . .

6.

She was not afraid that the homeland would kill her
but she was afraid that the homeland
would kill itself

7.

Like a cloud laden with poetry
she rained over my notebooks
wine . . . honey . . . and sparrows
red rubies
and sprinkled across my feelings
sails . . . and birds
and jasmine moons
After her departure
the age of thirst began
   the age of water came to an end

8.

I always felt that she was leaving
In her eyes, there were always sails
   being made for departure
airplanes crouching on her lashes
preparing to take off.
In her handbag—ever since I married her—
there was a passport . . . and an airplane ticket
visas to enter countries she had never visited

When I used to ask her:
And why do you have all these documents in
  your handbag?
She would answer:
because I have a date with a rainbow

9.

After they handed me her handbag
which they found under the rubble
and I saw her passport
the airplane ticket
the entry visas
I knew that I had not married Balqis Al-Rawi
but had married a rainbow ...

10.

When a beautiful women dies
the earth loses its balance
the moon declares mourning for a hundred years
and poetry becomes unemployed

11.

Balqis Al-Rawi
Balqis Al-Rawi
Balqis Al-Rawi
I used to love the cadence of her name
hold on to its ring
I used to fear attaching my name to it
in case I muddied the waters of the lake
and disfigured the beauty of the symphony

12.

It was not for this woman to live any longer
nor did she wish to live any longer
she is akin to the candles and lanterns
and like the poetic moment
she needs to explode before the last line. . . .

Fatima

Fatima refuses all texts whose authenticity is suspect
and begins from the first line
she tears up all the manuscripts written by males
and begins from the alphabet of her womanhood.
She throws away all her school books
and reads in the book of my lips.
Migrates from the cities of dust
and follows me barefoot to the cities of water.
Leaps out from the train of antiquity
and speaks with me the language of the sea
breaks her desert watch
and takes me with her outside of all time.

What Is Love?

What is love?
We have read a thousand treatises on it
and still do not know what we have read
read works of interpretation, astrology and medicine
and do not know where we began
we have memorized the whole of folk literature
poetry and song
and remember not a single line
we have asked the sages of love about their state
and discovered that they knew no more than we do

*

What is love?
We asked after it in its secret hiding place, but
each time we came to grasp it, it broke loose from us
we followed it through the forests, for years and years,
   but we lost our way
we pursued it to Africa . . . to Bengal
Nepal, the Caribbean, Majorca
and the jungles of Brazil
but never arrived
we asked love's wise men about their news
and discovered that they knew no more than we did

*

What is love?
We asked the saints about it, we asked the heroes of tales
they spoke the most beautiful words, but we were
   not convinced
once we asked our school mates about it
and they answered that it was a dreamy child
who wrote poetry about a narcissus
collected ants, nuts, and berries in its pinafore

and comforted abused kittens
we asked the experts on love about their experience
discovered that they knew no more than we did

*

What is love?
We asked the pious and the good about it ... but in vain
we asked men of religion ... but in vain
we asked lovers about it, and they said:
it left home as a child ...
carrying a bird and a branch in its hand
and we asked all its contemporaries about its age
they answered mockingly:
since when did love have an age?

*

What is love?
We heard that it was a divine decree
we believed what we had heard
and we heard that it was a heavenly star
so we opened the windows each night ... and sat waiting
we heard that it was lightning ... that if we touched it
    we would be electrified
we heard that it was a well-honed sword
that if we were to unsheathe it we would be slain
we asked the ambassadors of love about their travels
and discovered that they knew no more than we did

*

What is love?
We saw its face in the orchid ... but we did not
    understand
we heard its voice in the nightingale's cry ... yet we
    did not understand

glimpsed it atop a wheat stalk, in the deer's gait
in the colors of April
in the works of Chopin
but we did not notice
we asked the prophets of love about their secrets
and discovered that they knew no more than we did

*

And we turned to the princes of love in our history
we consulted with Laila's demented lover
we consulted with Lubna's demented lover
and discovered that they we called princes of love
were never happier than we were in their love.

*Poems Translated by
Lena Jayyusi and Christopher
Middleton*

Spanish Leaves

Spain

Spain!
weeping bridges
earth and sky

Sonata

Cry from the hollow
of its body:
the guitar sounds
death and birth of Spain

The Knight and the Rose

Spain—
   fans open
   combing the air,
innumerable black eyes
a hat flung from a lover's balcony,
and a voluptuous rose
flung from the women's quarter,
carrying in its petals hymns and prayers
for the knight of the South
in a red uniform,
who teases death,
armed only with a sword and his pride.

The House of Birds

In Seville
every beautiful woman
graces her hair
with a dark red flower
where every evening
all the birds of Spain
alight.

Fans

When spring has died on the hill
and summer's past,
what new blossoms flower
on a thousand brilliant fans.

Black Pearls

At noon the streets of Granada
are fields of black pearls
From where I sit

I see my country with wide eyes —
the minarets of Damascus
depicted on every braid of hair.

Doña Maria

With eyes wider than a desert
and features radiant with my native sun
and the sky-burst of its dawn horizons,
Doña Maria tears me apart;
I remember our house in Damascus
and its clear fountain lisping,
the lemon trees tall
and the old door on which I carved
My own love stories in untutored calligraphy
And now in your eyes, Doña Maria
I see my homeland again.

The Ambitious Earrings

Pendant from this beauty's ears
are thin earrings that chime
the way light vibrates in a crystal glass,
but no matter how searchingly they point
they cannot reach her bare shoulders.

The Bull (Toro, Toro)

In spite of the torrent of blood
and the arrows impaled in its flesh,
the noble victim's distinction
outlasts the victor's.

The Prophet's Blood

CORRIDA
CORRIDA
and the bull storms at the red banner,
powerful, obstinate,
and falls in the arena
like a martyr or prophet
he does not compromise his pride.

The Arabs' Relics

FLAMENCO
FLAMENCO
and the sleepy inn is wakened
by the clash of wooden cymbals
and a sad, husky voice
that issues like a gold fountain,
as I huddle in the corner
gathering the relics of the Arabs,
tears rushing to my eyes.

Andalusian Diary

In Spain
I had no need of inkwell or pen
to quench the thirst of paper
Morena Rossalia's eyes
scorched me with black desire
They were like two black inkwells
I voluptuously dipped into
They drank my life freely
like an Arab houdah

digging its fate on a distant horizon
digging its fate in my own.

*

Miranda Alafidra's dense hair
breathing like an African forest
is a long love story
I have known many such tales in my time
and how they have nibbled my life away!

*

The Spanish dancer
says everything with her fingers
involved in the only dance
where the finger becomes the mouth
The passionate call, eager assignations,
fury and appeasement, lust and fantasy—
a finger's crook tells all,
a finger's snap.

From where I sit
I'm obliterated by a symphony
of fingers

that lift me into an Andalusian skirt
rich with the hectic flowers of Spain
that blinds my eyes to the daylight
From where I sit
my twentieth glass secure in its place
the symphony of fingers is a tide
that recedes and rises
and the black rain falling from the eye's dilation
is something unknown in the history of rain
and eludes its memory
and I sit in my place
entreating the rain of black eyes
not to stop.

*

Analisa Donalia's
long earrings
are two stalactite tears
centuries ago they dropped from the ears
and haven't reached the shoulders' harbor
These and every pair of drop-earrings
worn by a Spanish woman are desperate attempts
to reach the fountain of light
that lives in the shoulders.

May your earrings never arrive,
Analisa Donalia,
and your journey be perpetual
Better to live in the light of illusion
than lie buried beneath such brilliant crystal.

O earrings of Analisa Donalia,
thirst of the light for the light.

*

Walking though Cordoba's narrow alleys
I kept searching my pockets, hoping to find
the key to our house in Damascus,
its beds of lilac, boxwood and cherry-plum,
the fountain's blue eye that looked at the house,
and the jasmine creeping on the bedroom's shoulder,
and the family's illustrious gold water-spout,
whose jet is inexhaustible,
the cool shaded colonnades,
everything that contributed
to my spiced childhood in Damascus
here I found it.

Dear lady, you who lean
against the wooden window,
don't be startled if I wash my hands
    in your little pool,
and pick a jasmine flower,
and climb the stairs to a small room,
an oriental room decorated with mother-of-pearl,
the sun extravagantly facing the window,
the lilac luxuriously mounting the curtain,
an oriental room
where my mother once set my bed.

You Write the Poems and I Sign Them

I have no power to change you
or explain your ways
Never believe a man can change a woman
Those men are pretenders
who think
that they created woman
from one of their ribs
Woman does not emerge from a man's ribs, not ever,
it's he who emerges from her womb
like a fish rising from depths of water
and like streams that branch away from a river
It's he who circles the sun of her eyes
and imagines he is fixed in place

*

I have no power to tame you
or domesticate you
or mitigate your first instincts
This task is impossible
I've tested my intelligence on you
also my dumbness
Nothing worked with you, neither guidance
   nor temptation
Stay primitive as you are

*

I have no power to break your habits
for thirty years you have been like this
for three hundred years
for three thousand
a storm trapped in a bottle
a body by nature sensing the scent of a man
assaults it by nature

triumphs over it by nature

Never believe what a man says about himself
that he is the one who makes the poems
and makes the children
It is the woman who writes the poems
and the man who signs his name to them
It is the woman who bears the children
and the man who signs at the maternity hospital
that he is the father

*

I have no power to change your nature
my books are of no use to you
and my convictions do not convince you
nor does my fatherly counsel do you any good
you are the queen of anarchy, of madness, of belonging
    to no one
Stay that way
You are the tree of femininity that grows in the dark
needs no sun or water
you are the sea princess who has loved all men
and loved no one
slept with all men ... and slept with no one
you are the Bedouin woman who went with all the tribes
and returned a virgin.
Stay that way.

The Perfume Seen, the Sound Inhaled

I soared in my imagination until
I made perfumes visible
and the echo's vibration fragrant.

The Swallow's Coat

My letters: the flocks of swallows trailing
their black coats across wakefulness.

Illusion

Gather your long hair ... this mad
disarray ... it frightens the night

I do not wish for charity, be a sash
of smoke, a date that never arrives

Do not come to our date ... leave me
in an illusion pitied by certainty.

Education

Your love taught me how love
changes the map of ages
taught me that when I love
the earth stops turning.

Sufi Revelations

When green mingles with black, with blue
with olive, with rose in your eyes, my lady
a rare condition takes hold of me
halfway between waking and absence, rapture and journey
between revelation and suggestion, death and birth
between the paper longing for love ... and the words.
Orchards beyond orchards beckon to me
gardens beyond gardens
lanterns beyond lanterns
and beyond them corners, cushions, disciples,
and children singing ... candles ... birthdays of saints
I see myself in a Damascus garden
surrounded by golden birds
and a golden sky
and fountains murmuring with voices of gold
and I see, as a man asleep sees, two open windows
behind which thousands of miracles take place

*

When at night the celebration of light and sound begins
in your eyes ... and all the minarets walk with joy
the mythical wedding begins, unlike any before it
and ships arrive from the Indies bearing you
   perfumes and suns,
then ...
passion lifts me up to seven heavens
that have seven gates
with seven sentries
every gate has seven compartments
with seven ladies-in-waiting
serving drinks in lunar goblets
and offering all who have died for love
the keys of eternal life

*

When the sea rises in your eyes like a green sword in
    the darkness
I am overcome by a wish to die, slain on the deck
    of a ship
distances beckon to me
lakes beckon
stars beckon
when the sea divides me in two
so that the moment of love becomes all moments
and water rushes madly from all directions
destroying all my bridges
erasing the details of my life
a craving to be gone takes hold of me
gone where there is a sea beyond the sea
beyond the ebb a flow ... beyond the flow and ebb
and beyond the sands gardens for all the faithful
and lighthouses
an unknown star
an unfamiliar love
an unwritten poem
and a breast ... never torn by the sword of a conqueror

*

When I enter the kingdom of rhythm, mint and water
do not hurry me
I may be overcome and shake like a dervish to the beat
    of drums
that call
when that happens
then, by God, my lady, do not wake me up
let me sleep on
    among the orchards, drunk on poetry and jasmine water
Perhaps in the night I will dream
I have become a lantern at the gate of a saint from
    Damascus

And I Do Not Protest

Why you?
Why you alone
of all women
change the geometry of my life
the rhythm of my days
steal, barefoot,
   into the world of my everyday affairs
   and lock the door behind you,
yet I do not protest?
Why is it
   I love precisely you,
   desire precisely you,
   choose precisely you,
and let you twist me
round your little finger
singing
smoking
playing cards,
yet I do not protest?

Why?
Why do you strike out all the ages
stop the motions of the centuries
kill the women of the tribe
within me
one ... by one
and I do not protest?

Why?
Why do I give you, of all women
the keys to my cities
that have never opened their gates
   to any tyrant
have never raised their white flags
   to any woman

and I ask my soldiers
to welcome you with anthems,
with waving kerchiefs
and victory crowns
and, to the sound of music and bells ringing
I declare you
before my citizens
a Princess for life?

A New Theory of the Origin of the World

In the beginning ... there was Fatima
After that the elements were formed
   fire and earth
   water and air
And then came the names and languages
   summer and spring
   morning and evening
After Fatima's eyes
the world discovered,
   the secret of the black rose
and then ... a thousand centuries later
other women came.

A Man's Nature

A man needs one minute
to love a woman
and centuries to forget her.

He Who Does Not Love You Remains Without a Homeland

I love you that I may remain bound
to God, to the land, to history, to time,
water, foliage, children when they laugh,
bread, sea, shells, ships,
night's star giving me its bracelets,
poetry that I inhabit, the wound that inhabits me.
You are the homeland that gives me identity
He who does not love you . . . has no homeland.

I Write

I write
to explode things; all writing is an explosion
I write
so that light will win over darkness
and the poem be a victory
I write
so that the wheat stalks will read me
and the trees will read me
I write
so that the rose will understand me,
   and the star, and the bird,
   and the cat, the fish, the shells and the oyster.

I write
to save this world from the dogteeth of Holako
from the rule of the militias
the madness of the leader of the gang
I write
to save women from the cells of tyrants
from the cities of the dead
from the state of polygamy
from the monotony of days
   the ice, the repetitiveness
I write
to save the word from the Inquisition
from the sniffing of dogs
the gallows of the censors.

I write
to save the woman I love
from the cities of no poetry,
   of no love
the cities of frustration and gloom
I write to make her a misty cloud

Only woman and writing
save us from death.

Love Compared

I do not resemble your other lovers, my lady
should another give you a cloud
   I give you rain
Should he give you a lantern, I
   will give you the moon
Should he give you a branch
   I will give you the trees
And if another gives you a ship
   I shall give you the journey.

My Sweetheart on the New Year

I love you
I do not want to link you with any memory of the past
nor with the memory of passing trains
you are the last train; night and day it travels
   across the veins of my hands
You are the last train
and I am your last station.

I love you
I do not wish to link you with water ... or wind
with the Muslim or Christian calendars
with the motion of ebb and flow
with the hours of solar and lunar eclipse
I do not care what the observatories say
nor the signs in the coffee cup
for your eyes alone are the prophecy
They alone are responsible
   for the joy in the world

When I Love

When I love
I feel that I am the king of time
I possess the earth and everything on it
and ride into the sun upon my horse.

*

When I love
I become liquid light
invisible to the eye
and the poems in my notebooks
become fields of mimosa and poppy.

*

When I love
the water gushes from my fingers
grass grows on my tongue
when I love
I become time outside all time.

*

When I love a woman
all the trees
run barefoot toward me . . .

Poems Translated by
Lena Jayyusi and Jeremy Reed

Death of Love

Decide what you wish,
but this is how it is, my dear,
without undue embellishment,
and pain pressing with urgency,
our love and hate are equalized,
and hanging on's no different from leaving.

My dear, we've read the morning papers twice,
and for a second time looked at the clock,
and as I recall we've shaken hands twice,
there's nothing more for us to do.
The ennui of the last two hours killed us,
I'm here, my nerves living on cigarettes,
while your hands turn cold in your loneliness.
I hope you'll come to understand
how birds of love never fly twice,
love, my friend, is a traveler
that visits us once only to depart.

Dedication

To a woman without an equal
who is called "City of my Sorrow"
to her who courses like a ship
through the water of my eyes
and enters—as I write—between me and my voice
I offer my death in the form of poetry,
how else, do you think, I can sing?

Love Will Remain My Master

I promised you
I'd disappear in five minutes
without a place to go?
the rain still sheeting in the streets
no place of refuge anywhere?
The city's coffee-bars define boredom,
where shall I embark on my own?
when you are the sea
   the sails
   and the journey
Is it possible for me to stay
   another ten minutes
   till the rain stops?
It's certain that I'll depart
   after the clouds move on
   and after the winds abate
Otherwise, I shall remain your guest
   until morning.

I See No One But You

It would be purposeless
to resist, or protest against your love
I and all my poems
are part of what your own hands fashioned
and it's an anomaly
to be surrounded by women
and see no one but you.

*

Loving you I arrived at the point of evanescence
the waters of the sea grew larger than the sea
tears of the eye outweighed the eye
and the stab wound leaves
a mark that encompasses the flesh.

*

I used to hear lovers
speak of their desire
and laugh,
but when I returned to my hotel
and drank my coffee alone
I discovered how a tormenting dagger enters
through the waist and never reappears.

*

If you know a man
who loves you more than I
guide me to him
so I may first congratulate
him on his constancy
and later, kill him.

An Arab Cure for Love

I thought your love no more
than a light rash on my skin
water or spirits would erase;
argued a difference in climate,
explained it by the change of seasons,
and when asked to account for it,
I blamed anxiety, sunstroke,
a hardly lasting light scratch on the face . . .

I thought your love a tributary
nursing the meadows, watering the fields,
but it invaded my inner terrain,
left drowned villages,
and flooded the land,
washed my bed away,
breached the walls of my house,
and left me stunned, standing in no-man's land.

At first I thought your love
would pass me like a cloud,
and that you were an anchorage,
a place of security,
and that our affair
would be resolved like all others—
you'd dissolve like writing on a mirror,
and time would be unsparing to roots we'd put down,
pack their vitality with snow.

I thought my passion for your eyes quite ordinary
my words of love like any other,
but now I see how my imagination fell short,
for your love was neither a rash
responsive to violet water and aniseed,
nor a scratch to be treated with herbal unguents,
nor a chill instigated by the North wind.

It was a sword dormant within my flesh,
an invading army,
the first stage on the road to madness.

Each Year That You Are My Beloved

Because I love you
the New Year greets us
with the stride of a king
and because of that love
I carry a special permit from God
to wander among the myriad stars.

*

May each year find you as my love
and I as your lover,
and if my wishes exceed all reason
my dreams transcend accepted bounds
who can admonish me for my fantasies?
it is no more than if a poor man dreams
that for five minutes, he is king,
or if we call the desert to account
for seeking life-enhancement of a stream?
Dream is legitimized by three conditions—
madness, poetry and the discovery
of an exceptional woman like you,
and it's my felicity
that I suffer from all three.

*

May your eyes always resemble Byzantine icons
and your breasts two golden-haired children
rolling over the snow
and may each year see our entanglement
and I pursued by the accusation of your love
as the sky is accused of blueness.

You Carry Time in Your Suitcase

What has become of you
Queen
who controlled the movements of the wind,
the fall of rain,
the height of the wheat stalk
the profusion of marguerites,
Queen
whose breasts fashioned the weather
and modulated
the ebb and flow
of seas across which boats voyaged
in search of ivory, wine
and pineapples.
What have you done with yourself
lady whose voice has fallen to the ground
and grown into a tree
and whose shadow has eclipsed my body
and become a fountain.
Why have you migrated from my breast
to choose homelessness,
why have you left the age of poetry
to elect a narrow time?
why have you broken the bottle of green ink
with which I used to draw you
and become a woman
in black
and white

Plan for Abducting a Woman I Love

As all years begin and end with you,
so at the outset of this one there's no need
for a declaration of my love for you
It would be laughable to do that,
for your presence is timeless
and you command the portals of the hours . . .

Beginning History

I hide no secret ... my heart's an open book
   not difficult for you to read
I date my life, beloved,
by the day I fell in love with you.

A Woman Walking Within Me

No one has read my coffee-cup
without divining you're my love,
nor studied the lines of my palm
and not discerned four letters of your name,
everything can be denied
except the fragrance of the one we love,
everything can be concealed
except a woman's footsteps moving within us,
everything can be debated
except your femininity.

What will become of us
in our comings and goings?
when all the coffee-bars have memorized our faces
and all the hotels registered our names
and the sidewalks grown accustomed to the music
  of our feet?
We're exposed to the world like a seaward balcony
visible like two goldfish
in a crystal bowl.

*Poems Translated by
Lena Jayyusi and
Naomi Shihab Nye*

Um Al-Mu'taz

(Elegy for my mother)

When Beirut was gasping in my arms
like a stabbed fish,
a call came from Damascus:
"Your mother has died."
At first I did not comprehend the words.
How could the fish be dying everywhere
at the same time?
The beloved city, Beirut,
the amazing mother, Fa'iza . . .
I emerged from one death
into another.
It was my destiny to travel between deaths.

My mother engaged in no public relations,
had not a single photograph in the archives of the press.
She attended no cocktail parties,
where birthday cakes are sliced in the glare
of flashbulbs and cellophane smiles.
She bought no clothes from London or Paris,
was never mentioned in social columns
or interviewed by any women's magazine,
which might have asked of her first love . . .
     first date . . . first man.
My mother was old-fashioned . . . she did not understand
how a woman could have a first love . . .
and a second . . . a third . . . or fifteenth.
My mother believed in one God, one lover, one love.

My mother's coffee was famous.
She ground it in her brass grinder, cup by cup,
boiling it over the coals and the flame of her patience.
She scented it with cardamom seed,
sprinkling two drops of orange blossom water
on the top.

In summers our balcony became
a rest-stop where men could drink
their morning coffee
before going to work.

With my mother's death
the last woolen shirt disintegrates
last shirt of tenderness
last umbrella held taut against
next winter—
you shall find me roaming the streets, naked.

Thus I Write the History of Women

I want you female as you are.
I claim no knowledge of woman's chemistry
The sources of woman's nectar
How the she-gazelle becomes a she-gazelle
Nor how birds perfect the art of song

*

I want you like the women
In immortal paintings
The virgins gracing
Cathedral ceilings
Bathing their breasts in moonlight
I want you female ... so the trees will sprout green
And the misty clouds will gather ... so that the rains will
come

*

I want you female because
Civilization is female
Poems are female
Stalks of wheat
Vials of fragrance
Even Paris—is female
and Beirut—despite her wounds—remains female
In the name of those who want to write poetry ... be a
woman
in the name of those who want to make love ... be a
woman
and in the name of those who want to know God ... be
a woman.

I Declare: There Is No Woman Like You

I declare
There is no other woman
Who can sweep through me like an earthquake
In moments of love
None but you
Who burns me, drowns me
Ignites and extinguishes me
Breaks me into two crescents . . . but you
No woman has preoccupied my soul
So long, so happily
Planted in me Damascus roses, mint and oranges
But you

Woman! Under whose hair I leave my questions
Who has never answered one of them . . .
You are all languages, yet
wordlessly sensed by the mind . . .
And never described.

I declare there is no other woman
Around whose waistline the ages gather
And a million stars revolve

I declare that only your arms
My beloved
Nurtured the first
And last male.

I declare
That no other woman emerges from the mist
When I smoke
Hovering like a white dove above my thoughts

Woman, on whom I wrote many a book
You have remained

More beautiful than all I wrote.

No other woman
Has sung to my body
Like a guitar
No other woman has elevated love
To prayer
But you.

I Love You

I love you thirty years each day
As I run this race
With my life
Time is too short for you
The minutes run
And chase after them
Somehow I feel I am establishing something
Planting something in the womb of the earth
Somehow I feel
When I love you
That I am transforming my time.

A Very Secret Report from Fist Country

Friends!
What is poetry if it does not declare mutiny?
If it does not topple tyrants?
What is poetry if it does not stir up volcanos where we
 need them?
And what is poetry if it cannot dislodge the crown
Worn by the powerful kings of this world?

An Unfinished Poem

What good is it to confess my experience in love?
People have always written of love,
Painting their stories on the walls of caves
On earthenware vases, engraved it on elephant tusks
    from India
Etched it on papyrus in Egypt
Or rice in China . . .
. . . Lavishing it with offerings and vows . . .

I am no priest nor teacher
I do not believe
Roses have to explain
Their fragrance to the world.
So what shall I write about?
This love is my experience alone
It is the sword piercing my solitude,
I am more present in death.

*

When I traveled your seas, my love,
I was not reading sea charts
I carried no rubber boat, no life buoy,
Approaching your blazing light
Like a Buddhist monk
Choosing my fate.
All I wanted
Was to scrawl my address across the sun
And build bridges over your breasts

*

When I loved you
I noticed the red cherries
In our orchard flamed like embers

The fish that escaped the children's hooks
Migrated to our shores in millions to lay their eggs
The cyprus trees grew taller
Life larger
And God
At last returned to the earth.

*

When I loved you
I noticed that summer came
Ten times each year
Wheat grew wildly
In our fields each day
The moon that had fled our town
Returned to rent a house and a bed
And arak brewed with sugar and anise
Was more delicious.

*

When I tried to write of my love
I suffered hell
I felt the burden of the
Whole sea on my back
A weight known only to those
Lost for ages
In the depths.

*

What should I write about your love, my dear?
The only thing I remember is
Waking up one morning
To find myself a prince.

*

Try to understand
The birds of love do not fly twice
Love is a traveler
That visits only once ... then departs.

To a Swiss Friend

Friend, writing is a curse
Escape, then, from my stormy hell!
I had thought the copybooks were my refuge
but discovered that poetry is killing me.
I had thought your love would end my estrangement
but you passed like water between my fingers

Once I preached the religion of love but
canaries were snuffed out in a moment.
In the cities of dust there's no difference
Between the picture of a poet and a broker.

God, there's a shore for every wound
But my wounds have no shores!
No country heals the desolation of one
Whose greatest exile is within his soul.

Drink your coffee
Listen quietly to my words
Perhaps we will not drink coffee together ever again
And I will have no other chance to speak.

I shall not speak of you
Nor of myself
We are two zeros in relation to love
Two lines scrawled in pencil on its margin
But I shall speak
Of something bigger and purer
Than either of us

This amazing butterfly
Which lit on our shoulders but we flicked it away
This golden fish
Which rose from the depth of the sea
And we crushed it.

This blue star
Which extended its light to us
And we extinguished it
It is not a matter of your taking your suitcase and going
Many women hoist their bags in moments of anger
And go
It is not a matter of my stubbing out this cigarette
    irritably
On the seat cover
Many men burn seat covers when they are angry.
It is not that simple
It concerns neither of you . . . not I
Two zeros in relation to love
Two lines scrawled in pencil on its margin.
The matter concerns this golden fish . . .
Which the sea one day threw to us
And we crushed between our fingers.

Love Does Not Stop at the Red Light

Fatima of the Place de la Concorde,
Queen of all Fatimas
Figure like a sword bejeweled with elegant script
Waist encircled with song,
Language that dissolves all other languages,
I welcome you to Paris,
I wish you a happy stay
grazing my body's terrain.
Arab woman, whose eyes drip black honey
whose lips seep quiet
Even your earrings chime out Sunday mornings
Like steeples of bells
I never expected that one day
I would pass with you
beneath the Arc de Triomph
to place a rose on the grave of the unknown lover.
Fatima:
Mouth of cardamom perfume,
Pastel painted feet,
I never expected to be
The most famous lover in the history of the Arabs
and the history of France
I never expected
to enter Paris with an Arab passport
and leave it
President of the fifth republic!!

125

Say I Love You

Say I love you . . .
So I may grow beautiful
Say I love you . . . that my fingers may turn
into gold and my forehead become a lantern
Say I love you that my transformation may be complete
    and I become
a wheatstalk or palm tree
Say it now, do not hesitate
some loves bear no postponement
Say I love you that my saintliness increase and
    my poetry of
love become a holy book
I would change the calendar should you wish it
erase seasons, add extra seasons
the old ear defunct in my hands
I would establish the kingdom of women.

Say I love you that my poems might become
fluid and my writings divine.
Were you my lover I might
invade the sun with horses and ships.
Don't be shy . . . this is my only chance
to become a god . . . or a prophet.

A Lesson in Drawing

My son places his paint box in front of me
and asks me to draw a bird for him.
Into the color gray I dip the brush
and draw a square with locks and bars.
Astonishment fills his eyes:
" ... But this is a prison, Father,
Don't you know, how to draw a bird?"
And I tell him: "Son, forgive me,
I've forgotten the shape of birds."

*

My son puts the drawing book in front of me
and asks me to draw a wheatstalk.
I hold the pen
and draw a gun.
My son mocks my ignorance,
demanding,
"Don't you know, Father, the difference between a
    wheatstalk and a gun?"
I tell him, "Son,
Once I used to know the shape of wheatstalks
the shape of the loaf
the shape of the rose
But in this hardened time
the trees of the forest have joined
the militia men
and the rose wears dull fatigues
In this time of armed wheatstalks
armed birds
armed culture
and armed religion
you can't buy a loaf
without finding a gun inside
you can't pluck a rose in the field

127

without its raising its thorns in your face
you can't buy a book
that doesn't explode between your fingers."

*

My son sits at the edge of my bed
and asks me to recite a poem.
A tear falls from my eyes onto the pillow.
My son licks it up, astonished, saying:
"But this is a tear, father, not a poem!"
And I tell him:
"When you grow up, my son,
and read the *diwan* of Arabic poetry
you'll discover that the word and the tear are twins
and the Arabic poem
is no more than a tear wept by the writing fingers."

*

My son lays down his pens, his crayon box in
    front of me
and asks me to draw a homeland for him.
The brush trembles in my hands
and I sink, weeping.

Wheatstalk That Emerges

Ah . . . wheatstalk watered with tears,
the sword has entered the heart, we cannot return.
Poised at love's dangerous gate
I love you on the knife's silvery blade
to the point of death and trembling.
We are too much known —
history illuminates me
and rumors increase . . .
This is what always happens in great relationships.

Ah, Fatima,
you with whom I have shared thousands
of small acts of foolishness,
I know what it means to be in love
behind the walls of Arabian time
I know what it means to pledge,
to whisper and declare, in this
Arabian time
and I know what it means for you to be mine
throughout this era's terror.

The police summon me for interrogation
The color of your eyes, what lies beneath my shirt
and in my heart
my trips, my thoughts, my latest poems.
Should they catch me
inscribing the kohl that rains down from your eyes
their rifles would follow me.
Loosen your hair
for the solitary man
persecuted like a prophet
Loosen your hair, remove the clips,
this may be our last chance.

Ah, exquisite icon of my life,

each morning you pull me back
to the playgrounds of childhood
impossible suns bloom beneath your eyelids
impossible countries materialize
You mythical treasure that accompanied me
on trains going north,
the ink of China in your eyes
precedes my ancestry,
you pass through my veins
like orange perfume.

At night you cleave me in two
and at sunrise cast me across your knees,
   a crescent moon.
You occupy me east and west, right and left—
such pleasant occupation!
I miss our days at Lake Windermere
when I longed to walk with you on the water,
the clouds, to walk across time,
and weep on your breast forever.
I long for the country pubs,
our seats by the fire,
for all the white peaks
when the kohl of Hijaz mingles with snow
I long for cognac
in the chilling night.

Ah, water bird perched beside me
on northern trains,
grasp me tightly by the arm.
The decrees of Sultans and files of police
mean nothing to me.
Your love, alone, preoccupies.
We have gambled much and trespassed far
beyond the realm of traffic lights.
Grasp my arm so the earth may turn . . .
without a great love, the earth does not turn.

130

Friends of Poetry!

I am the tree of fire, and priest of longing,
the spokesman for fifty million lovers.
The people of yearning sleep in my arms
And sometimes I make doves for them
And sometimes jasmine trees.
Friends,
I am the wound forever refusing
The authority of the knife!

Poems Translated by
Sharif Elmusa and Jeremy Reed

The Interrogation

Who killed the Imam?
The sleuths criss-cross my room.
Who killed the Imam?
The soldier's boots work on my neck.
Who killed the Imam?
Who stabbed the dervish
and ripped the caftan,
tore off the amulets
and the decorative rosary?
It's unnecessary
to pull out my fingernails
for evidence,
what happened is manifest
in the dead body.

*

Who killed the Imam?
Enter, soldiers armed to the teeth.
Exit, soldiers armed to the teeth.
Reports, taperecorders, photographers.
Tell me, of what use is my testimony,
your report is written
whether I speak or keep silent.
What is the point of my begging for mercy?
You'll strike me regardless
of my help or restraint.
Since you first governed this land
you've abrogated my freedom of thought.

*

I'm neither, contrary to your expectations,
a communist nor a rightist.
I was born in Damascus,

135

a city I'm sure you don't know exists,
for you've not quenched your thirst at its waters,
or known the frenzy of its love.
Not in a single flower-market
will you find a rose like Damascus,
not in all the jewelers' windows
a pearl so inimitable,
nor in any city find
the sad eyes of my own.

*

I'm not an insidious agent
as alleged by your informants.
I've never stolen a grain of wheat,
killed an ant or entered a jail.
Everyone knows me in my district,
both child and adult, dove and tree,
I'm known to all God's prophets,
I say my prayers five times a day,
never omitting the Friday sermon,
and for twenty years I've performed
the prescribed rituals of the prayers,
and, in everything, imitated his highness, the Imam.
He says, "God may obliterate Israel,"
and, I repeat his sentiment.
He says, "God, may you scatter that nation,"
and I affirm his words.
He says, "God, may you flood their harvest,"
and I reiterate his desire;
my repetition's endless.
And for twenty years
I've lived in a sheep-pen,
slept like a sheep,
urinated likewise,
taken fodder like sheep,
twirled like a bead in the Imam's rosary,

136

parroting his injunctions
without a mind of my own
without a head
or feet,
sniffing the cold from his beard
and consumption from his bones.
I've spent twenty years
heaped like a bundle of straw on the red prayer rug,
whipped every Friday by a blazing sermon,
swallowing the rhetoric, the trope
and the precious poem.
For twenty years, sirs,
I've lived in a mill
that grinds only air.

*

It was with the dagger that you see,
I stabbed the Imam in the chest and neck,
knifed him in his termited brain,
murdered him in my own name
and that of a million reiterative sheep.
I know my penalty justifies death,
but in killing him I also killed
all the roaches that sing in the dark
and those who lie on the sidewalks of dreams,
and the conglomerate who, for a thousand years,
have misapplied words;
I killed the beggars from the store of Islam
and all the drones in its garden.

An Invitation for the Fifth of June

(on the fifth anniversary of the Arab defeat in June 1967)

You come back for the fifth year,
barefoot, a burlap sack slung on your back,
the sadness of the heavens mapped on your face—
so, too, the pain of Job,
and we'll greet you at every airport
with bouquets, and drink your health with copious wine.
We'll sing and recite insincere poems in your presence,
and you'll get used to us
and we to you.

*

We ask you to vacation here in summer,
like all tourists,
and we'll designate you the royal suite
prepared especially for you.
You may enjoy the night... and the neon lights,
the rock and roll, the porno and the jazz—
here we know only felicity,
and in my country you'll find what pleases,
furnished flats for lovers,
abundance of liquor,
and a harem for the caliph.

Why are you so curtailed in flight?
My sad-faced guest,
we have streams and grass and beautiful girls,
so why your diffidence?
We'll help you forget Palestine,
and pluck the tear-tree from your eyes,
and from the Qur'an erase the verses,

the "Compassionate" and the "Conquest,"
and we'll assassinate Jesus Christ
and grant you an Arab passport
that has no return visa.

*

Fifth year
sixth
seventh
eighth
ninth
tenth year
what do the years amount to?
All our grand cities, from the Euphrates to the Nile,
are lost now to memory.
We've forgotten the men who disappeared in the desert
and those who died are extinguished.
What do the years count for?
We've prepared the funeral wreaths and the scarves
and composed the orations,
and carved, a week before your arrival,
the marble of the tombstones.
O East that feeds on the paper of communiques
and trails like a lamb behind posters
O East that writes the name of its fallen
on the faces of mirrors
on the waists of belly dancers—
what do the years count for?
What ever do they amount to?

139

Beirut Is Your Pleasure Woman, Beirut Is My Love

Forgive us
if we left you to die alone
if we slipped out like runaway soldiers,
pardon us
if we watched you bleed carnelian rivers
and saw adultery performed
but remained silent.

*

Tell me you're well,
Beirut in your sadness.
Has the sea too
been killed by a sniper's bullet?
And love?
Is it now a refugee ... among the thousands?
And poetry?
After you Beirut can there still be poetry?
The futility of war has left us butchered,
emptied us of our substance,
scattered our people to the four corners —
pariahs, wasting.
It has left us, against all prophecy, as lost Jews.

*

They asked us to train as gunmen,
and we declined,
they proposed we divide God in half,
we encountered shame.
We believe in God,
why have they denied him a meaning?
They asked us to testify against love

140

but we wouldn't bear witness,
they proposed we curse Beirut
which fed us love and wheat,
provided us with tenderness.
We declined to sever the breast
which had nurtured us.
We opposed the gunmen
and took the side of Lebanon . . . mountain and valley,
and took the side of Lebanon . . . cross and crescent,
and supported Lebanon's fountains and springs,
country of clustering grapes and passion,
and we upheld the place with taught us poetry
and gave us the gift of writing.

*

We suffered our exile for twenty months
and drank our tears throughout that time
and hunted everywhere for a new love,
but could not love,
and drank wine from all the grapevines
but never grew intoxicated
and looked for a substitute
great Beirut
good Beirut
pure Beirut.
We found none.
We came back and kissed the ground
whose very stones make poetry,
and embraced you, field and birds, sun and corniche,
and screamed like madmen thronging a ship's deck,
only you Beirut . . . there's no other in the world!

Beirut, Mistress of the World

Beirut, mistress of the world—
who sold your ruby bracelets,
confiscated your magic ring,
and cut the golden braids?
Who extinguished the radiance
that slept in the green of your eyes?
Who scratched your face with a knife
and sprayed acid on your perfect lips?
Who poisoned the sea
and disseminated hate on the rosy coast?
We are here with an apology, and a confession—
we opened fire on you, in a tribal spirit,
and killed a lady who was once called
Liberty.

*

What can we say, Beirut,
when your eyes are forced to bear
the essence of man's grief,
while the civil war strews ash
on your burnt breast?
Who would have thought
we'd meet you in ruins, Beirut,
or that the flower would grow a thousand fangs,
the eye oppose its eyelashes?

What can we say, my pearl, my stalk of wheat,
my pen, my dream, my book of verse?
Where have you contracted such cruelty
after ineffable tenderness?
I can't see how the sparrow's been transformed
into a wild cat; you've forgotten God
and returned to pagan ways.

142

*

Rise from beneath the blue wave, Ishtar,
like a poem composed of roses and flame.
Nothing comes before or after you,
nor withstands comparison.
You're the essence of all time,
field of pearls, love's harbor, peacock of water.
Rise for the sake of love and poets,
and in the interests of poverty.
Love seeks you, prettiest of queens—
look how you, paid, like all beautiful women,
the price of beauty
and the penalty of free speech.

*

Beirut, mistress of the world,
city of first love, first promise,
where I wrote my poems and concealed
them in velvet bags—
We now confess, Beirut,
that we loved you like nomads
and made love to you in their fashion.
You were our pleasure woman,
nightlong we took refuge in your bed
and in the morning scattered.
We realize now we were illiterate and blind
and instrumental in your fall.
We watched your head fly like a bird
down the Rock of Rowsheh into the sea.
We admit that when your sentence
was implemented, we stood by as false witnesses.

*

We confess before the one God

that we were jealous of you,
your beauty hurt us.
It's clear our misunderstanding wronged you,
presented you with a knife for a rose,
we seduced you slept with you
and used you as a scapegoat for our sins.

Mistress of the world,
after your beauty nothing compensates,
we come to the knowledge too late
of your rootedness in our souls,
we now know our crime.

God searches the map for paradise in Lebanon,
and the sea looks in its blue notebook for that name,
and the green moon
has returned to marry that country.
Give me your hand, star of the night,
lily of all cities. We must now confess
we were sadists, our rapacity
followed the devil's bidding.
Beirut, mistress of the world,
rise from the rubble
   like an almond blossom in April,
rise from your grief,
revolution is born of tragedy.
Rise in honor of woods and rivers
in homage to Man.
We sinned, Beirut,
   and ask your forgiveness.

*Poems Translated by
Sharif Elmusa and Naomi
Shihab Nye*

Children Bearing Rocks

With mere rocks in their hands,
they stun the world
and come to us like good tidings.
Bursting with love and anger,
they defy, and topple,
while we remain a herd of polar bears
bundled against weather.

Like mussels we sit in cafés,
one hunts for a business venture
one for another billion
a fourth wife
breasts polished by civilization.
One stalks London for a lofty mansion
one traffics in arms
one seeks revenge in nightclubs
one plots for a throne, a private army,
a princedom.

Ah, generation of betrayal,
of surrogate, indecent men,
generation of leftovers,
we'll be swept away—
never mind the slow pace of history—
by children bearing rocks.

147

Jerusalem

Jerusalem, luminous city of prophets,
shortest path between heaven and earth!

Jerusalem, you of the myriad minarets,
become a beautiful little girl with burned fingers.
City of the Virgin, your eyes are sad.
Shady oasis where the Prophet passed,
the stones of your streets grow sad,
the towers of mosques downcast.
City swathed in black, who'll ring the bells
at the Holy Sepulchre on Sunday mornings?
Who will carry toys to children
on Christmas Eve?
City of sorrows, a huge tear
trembling on your eyelid,
who'll save the Bible?
Who'll save the Qur'an?
Who will save Christ, who will save man?

Jerusalem, beloved city of mine,
tomorrow your lemon trees will bloom,
your green stalks and branches rise up joyful,
and your eyes will laugh. Migrant pigeons
will return to your holy roofs
and children will go back to playing.
Parents and children will meet
on your shining streets,
my city, city of olives and peace.

Honorary Doctorate in the Chemistry of Stone

1.

He throws one stone or two
and slices Israel's snake in half.
He gnaws on the flesh of tanks
and returns to us without hands.
In moments only,
a country appears on the clouds,
a homeland in the eyes.
In moments only,
Haifa appears, Jaffa appears,
Gaza rides the sea,
and Jerusalem lights up
like a minaret.

2.

He paints a horse from the rubies of dawn
and enters riding, like Alexander the Great.
He wrenches off the doors of history,
severs the era of hashish smokers,
closes the pimp bazaar,
and casts off the primitive past.
In moments only
the olive trees conceive
and milk flows in the breasts.
He draws a land in Tiberius
and plants wheat. He draws a house on Mount Carmel,
a mother grinding coffee beans by the door,
and two waiting cups.
In moments only the fragrance of lemon blossoms
    assails us
and a homeland is born in the eyes.

3.

Perhaps he casts a moon from his black eyes,

maybe two.
He throws his pen, books, ink,
his drawing pads, glue, and paintbrushes.
Maryam shouts, "Ah, my son!"
and embraces him as a little boy falls.
In that moment
a thousand boys are born,
a Gaza moon is eclipsed,
and a new moon rises in Bisan.
In that moment a country steps into a prison cell,
and a homeland is born in the eyes.

4.

He shakes the sand off his shoes
and enters the kingdom of water.
He unfurls a new horizon,
creating a different age,
and writes a new text
penetrating the desert's memory.
He erases the hackneyed rhetoric
from A to Z,
breaking a hole in its dictionary,
announcing the death of tyranny
and all our grand demonstrative poems.

5.

With one thrown stone
Palestine's face begins forming
like its own poem.
With the second stone
Acca floats on the water, rhythmically.
With the third, Ramallah emerges
from the night of misery, like a fragrant violet.
The boy throws the tenth stone
so the face of God may appear
lighting the dawn.

150

6.
Important newspapers inquire:
"Who's this new prophet from Canaan?
Who is this boy born from the womb of grief?
What mythical plant is this
twining from the walls?
What ruby colored rivers spring forth
from the leaves of the Qur'an?"
Clairvoyants, mystics, Buddhists,
kings, and the *djinn* ask about him.
"Who is this boy sprouting like red plums
from the trees of forgetfulness?
Who is this boy erupting
from his ancestors' pictures
and a generation's lies?
Who is this boy looking for
the flowers of love,
the sun of men?
Who is this boy with eyes blazing
like a Greek god's?"

7.
Now storytellers write about him,
travelers tell his tale.
A boy abandoning the usual childhood illnesses,
the mothworm that nibbles words . . .
Who is he? This boy who leapt forth
from the moldering compost of patience
and the language of the dead . . .
World newspapers ask how a little boy,
lovely as a rose, can change the world,
American newspapers ask
how a boy from Gaza or Haifa,
Acca or Nablus,
can take his school eraser
and overturn the giant truck of history
on the ancient road!

151

The Visa

I stood for inspection
at the Security Office at the frontier of a developing
    country.
I had nothing on me but my sorrows.
With my country just one mile away,
my heart flapped within my ribs
like a pigeon yearning for water.
In my hand, my passport,
and I dreamed of that land
that had fed me with its wheat, almonds and figs,
in whose nurturing fields I had played.

In the long line
People were eating melon seeds and *turmus*
and pissing like sheep.
Since the times of the pharaohs till now
there's always been a despotic ruler
and a people pissing on themselves like sheep.

*

At a security post in my Arab world
(not in the Congo, nor Tanzania)
the sun was wearing khaki
the trees wore khaki
and the rose wore its own fatigues.
Fear stood in line in front of us,
and behind.
An officer armed with five stars and his hatred
dragged us like animals behind him.
Since the days of Abel till now
there has always been a professional killer
and a people flayed like cattle.

*

At the torture post where sun and time never revolve
where nothing remains of men except rind and leaf
a red line stretched.
Between two Berlins, two Beiruts, two Sanaas
two Meccas, two Qur'ans, two sects
two dialects,
two quarters,
two traffic signs.
Terror was the king of seasons,
the earth had been begging for rain since September
and we were begging the royal order to Enter.

*

Where am I?
Between one street and another
    a country is created
Between one wall and another
    a country is created
Between each palm and the next
    a country is created
Between a woman and her child
    a country is created
O Creator! You who have drawn out the horizons
and engineered the sky
is that little hole which cannot be seen
also a country?

*

At the post of madness, headache, coughing and
    sicknesses,
I stood a whole month
    a whole year
    a whole century

at the door of the Mafia chief
begging him for permission to cross
begging him for the
home of my childhood
begging him for the roses, the lilies, the dahlias
begging him for my room
for the ink, the pens, and chalk
As I faced the Soviet guns I asked myself

is it possible
God has become the chief of the Mafia?

*

At a nameless post of fear
which grows and grows
I became an old old man
By this time they had agreed I could enter my own
   country
but I knew that the homeland which I had loved
is no more a part of geography
no more a part of geography
no more a part of geography.

Elegy for Nasir

We have killed you, last of the prophets,
you are dead! It isn't new,
this killing of prophets and saints.
How many an imam has been murdered
as he performed his evening prayers!

You came to us, a beautiful book
we didn't know how to read.
You invited us to the land of innocence
but we refused to follow.
We left you alone in the Sinai sun,
naked and thirsty, murmuring to your God,
while we went on selling slogans to the stupid,
feeding masses with hay and straw
leaving them to gnaw on air.

Mountain of pride, we've killed you,
the last oil lamp who could have lighted
our winter nights, we've killed you
with both of our hands and blamed it
on fate!

Beloved friend, father, when we washed
our hands, we found we had killed our hopes
and the blood on the pillow was our own!

You shook the dust of dervishes from our skin
returning us to our youth,
you accompanied us to the land of the impossible,
teaching us pride and strength,
but when the trip proved too long,
we murdered our horse.

We brought you our deformities,
our digressions, our resentments,

we slaughtered you with the sword
of our sorrows!
I wish you had never appeared in our land,
I wish you had been the prophet
of another people.

Abu Khalid, the poem you were
made ink sprout leaves.
Where did you go, horseman of dreams?
What good is any race when the steed is dead?
All myths died with your death,
Sheherezad committed suicide,
behind your funeral procession all Quraish marched.
There was Hisham, and Ziyad—
princes with hidden daggers shedding tears.
One prince still wakes from dreams trembling.
Another tries to be king like you were
but after you, all kings are ash.

I call upon you, Abu Khalid,
hear my wail. I know my scream
echoes deep in a valley
and you will never answer me.
Miracles don't repeat themselves.

Posters

You will not do to our people
what's been done to the Native Americans
for here we shall stay
on this land that wears
a bracelet of flowers on its wrist
This is our country
Since the dawn of time we've lived in it,
played and loved in it, and breathed our poetry
We are rooted strong in its bays as seaweed,
rooted in this history of breads and olives
and yellowing corn,
rooted in its conscience
and we will stay for March, for April,
stay like carvings on crosses,
stay, with the noble prophet, the Qur'an,
and the Ten Commandments . . .

Don't get drunk with victory
for if you kill Khalid, Amr will come
and if you crush a rose,
its fragrance will remain

From the reeds of forests
we will emerge, liked *jinn*, to meet you
from postal packages, bus seats,
from gravestones and cigarette boxes
from gasoline cans, chalk, blackboards and braids
from the wood of crosses, from incense burners
from prayers scarves
from the pages of the Qur'an we shall come
from its lines and verses
You will not escape us
for we inhabit the wind, the water, the plants
we are kneaded into crayons and voices
You will not escape

157

never escape, from the Nile to the Euphrates

Nor will you rest;
every slain one amongst us
dies a thousand times

Children of Israel, do not be deceived!
The hands of the clock, no matter how many
    times stopped,
will revolve again . . .
Seizing of land does not frighten us,
nor long thirst—
feathers have not abandoned eagles' wings
water remains at the heart of stones.
You defeated armies, not feelings
You cut off trees
but their roots remain

You stole a whole homeland
and the world clapped for the adventure
You confiscated thousands of our homes
and sold our children into sorrow
You've stolen oil from our churches
and Christ from his home in Nazareth
and the world clapped for an adventure
yet you hold a wake
if we hijack a plane

Always remember that
America the Strong
is not God Almighty
America the Powerful
cannot prevent birds from flying
A big man can be killed
by a rifle a child holds

What's between you and us

158

does not end in a year
or five years or ten or even a thousand
The battle for liberation is long as a fast
and we will remain engraved in your chests
like carving in stone
We will keep our home in the voice of waterpipes
and wings of doves, in the memory of the sun
and the copybook of days
We shall remain in children's mischief
and pencil scribbles
as in the poetry of our greatest bards
Find us on the lips of those we love
in something simple as pronunciation

Grief's children will grow up
as will the children of this long extended pain
The martyrs of Palestine have children who are
  growing up
as do neighborhoods, soil, and doors
Those you have gathered the past thirty years
in police stations, prisons, rooms for interrogation
are gathering somewhere like tears in an eye
and at any moment through all the gates of Palestine
will arrive

After my long journey replete with suffering
and rampant with mirages
I, the Palestinian, emerge like grassblades
from a ruin
I gleam like lightning on your faces
falling like rain every single night
from the mouths of yards, from door handles,
from mulberry leaves and ivy bushes,
from the quiet pond and the chattering of waterpipes
I emerge
from my father's voice
and my mother's gentle face

from every black eyelash
the letters between lovers
and the beloved's window
even from the smell of dust
I open the door of my home
and enter again, without waiting
for an answer
because I am the question and the answer